# What is ecology?

Every living thing that is known to exist is found on one planet, the Earth. They all share this planet, from bacteria too small to be seen without a microscope to the giant redwood trees and the whales of the oceans.

All the living and non-living things that surround such a plant or animal are called its environment. For example, the environment of a plant includes the soil, the water and foodstuffs in the soil and the air the plant is growing in. Rainfall and temperature may affect the life of the plant as well as other plants that may compete for water and food. There may also be animals that eat the plant and some that may help it to reproduce. All these things make up the plant's environment. The science that looks at the ways in which plants and animals affect their environment, and are affected by it, is called "ecology."

# LAND ECOLOGY

Jennifer Cochrane

**Series Consultant: John Williams, C.Biol., M.I.Biol.**
**Series Illustrator: Cecilia Fitzsimons, B.Sc., Ph.D.**

**The Bookwright Press**
**New York · 1987**

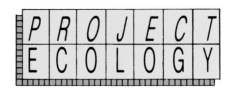

**Air Ecology**
**Animal Ecology**
**Land Ecology**
**Plant Ecology**
**Urban Ecology**
**Water Ecology**

First published in the
United States in 1987 by
The Bookwright Press
387 Park Avenue South
New York, NY 10016

First published in 1987 by
Wayland (Publishers) Ltd
61 Western Road, Hove
East Sussex BN3 1JD, England

© Copyright 1987 Wayland (Publishers) Ltd

Typeset in the UK by
DP Press Ltd, Sevenoaks, Kent
Printed in Italy by
G. Canale & C.S.p.A., Turin

ISBN 0–531–18153–7
Library of Congress Catalog Card Number:
86–73061

Cover: bottom *weeding rice paddies in Japan,* left *the Arches National Park in Utah,* right *Sun-cracked ground by the Blue Nile in the Sudan, Africa.*

Frontispiece: *Animal remains on the cracked earth of a dried up lagoon in Australia.*

# Contents

# 1. The Earth below us

All living things need the minerals that are contained in the thin, solid layer of rock that covers the planet. These "nutrients" are dissolved from the rock, and plants take them in to make their food. The animal life, in turn, relies on the plants as the source of food, so the land is truly essential for life. Indeed, the calcium in your teeth and bones and the iron in your blood came originally from the rocky crust of the planet.

This crust is made up of two layers. The upper layer is called sial after its main ingredients: silicon and aluminum. The sial may be up to 40 km (25 mi)thick under the oceans and is thicker under high mountain ranges. This layer floats on a denser layer called sima, which contains mainly silicon and magnesium. The sial does not totally cover the sima but makes up the great land masses, called the continents, while the sima is found on the bed of the oceans.

Below the crust is a layer called the mantle, reaching down some 2,900 km (1,800 mi)to the core, which is the extremely dense innermost part of the Earth. The temperature increases as we travel down through the layers to the core, up to about 4,000°C (7,200°F) at the center. The temperature and pressure is such that some of the rock in the lower part of the crust and the upper part of the mantle melts, making magma. It is this magma that rises up to the surface through cracks in the crust during a volcanic eruption.

*A section through the Earth's crust to show the layers.*

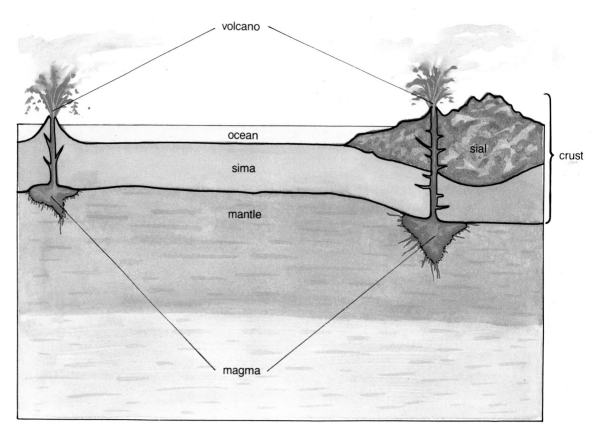

Most volcanoes and earthquakes are found where there are cracks in the Earth's crust. These cracks are actually the boundaries between huge blocks called "plates." The crust and the top part of the mantle are divided into several massive plates, each of which is moving. Where two plates touch there is violent activity like volcanoes.

So, the continents have not always been in the positions that we know so well from maps of the world. Some 200 million years ago all

*A river of lava in the Galapagos Islands.*

the land was together in one huge continent called Pangaea. This land broke up and the plates drifted apart, very slowly, to reach their present positions. If you compare the east coast of South America and the west coast of Africa you can see how they once fitted together. There are even the impressions (called fossils) of the same creatures in rocks from both continents.

# 3. Crumbling the rocks

Soils are created partly by the breaking down of rocks into small particles. This is called weathering. Mechanical weathering includes the action of water, wind and temperature changes on the rock.

In wet, mountainous areas the cracks in rocks are filled with water. When water freezes it expands so that the ice takes up more space. The cracks are then made wider by the freezing process, eventually splitting the rock. The particles of rock in water will cause further weathering in the path of streams and rivers.

In dry places the rocks are heated to high temperatures during the day. When the Sun sets, though, the temperature falls quickly and the rapid cooling cracks the rock. The wind-driven soil will also scour the surface of rocks, like a sandblaster.

Plants and animals add to the weathering. For example, young trees will often take root in cracks in the rock. As the tree grows the pressure will force the rock apart.

Chemical weathering will also have an effect. Rainwater is a complex substance containing dissolved carbon dioxide, which turns into a weak acid (carbonic acid). This is natural acid rain. Limestone is made up mostly of calcium carbonate, which will not dissolve in pure water. However, the natural acid rain reacts with the calcium carbonate to give calcium bicarbonate, which will dissolve and be taken away in the water. The giant caves found within areas of limestone are caused by this.

*Wherever gritty particles are blown against rock surfaces there will be some erosion. This is particularly so in desert areas such as here in the Arches National Park, Utah.*

Most volcanoes and earthquakes are found where there are cracks in the Earth's crust. These cracks are actually the boundaries between huge blocks called "plates." The crust and the top part of the mantle are divided into several massive plates, each of which is moving. Where two plates touch there is violent activity like volcanoes.

So, the continents have not always been in the positions that we know so well from maps of the world. Some 200 million years ago all

*A river of lava in the Galapagos Islands.*

the land was together in one huge continent called Pangaea. This land broke up and the plates drifted apart, very slowly, to reach their present positions. If you compare the east coast of South America and the west coast of Africa you can see how they once fitted together. There are even the impressions (called fossils) of the same creatures in rocks from both continents.

# 2. The stony skeleton

Inside each of the two layers of the Earth's crust, the sial and the sima, there are three basic kinds of rock.

Some of the rocks are formed when the molten rock wells up to the surface through the crust and cools to become solid. We can see this happening today when a volcano erupts. The molten lava flows out of the crater and quickly turns to solid rock. The minerals in the magma quickly turn into small crystals. Some magma cools slowly underground and the crystals that form are larger and can be easily seen in rocks such as basalt. These are examples of what are called igneous rocks.

The second group of rocks are called sedimentary rocks. These were formed when particles of sand, soil and mud were pressed into layers on lake or seabeds to give rocks such as sandstone and shale.

Some sedimentary rocks are made from the

*These pillars of igneous basalt rock were created by the rapid cooling of lava as it flowed into the sea. They form the "Giant's Causeway" in Northern Ireland.*

remains of once living things. Coal is formed from the remains of plants that grew in swamps and were changed over millions of years. Limestone may be formed from the shells of sea creatures such as tiny one-celled animals and snails and cockles. The fossils of long-dead creatures and plants may be found in sedimentary rocks.

The third group of rocks are called metamorphic rocks. These are "altered" rocks, formed when heat, pressure and sometimes chemical changes turn igneous and sedimentary rocks into different ones. For example, heat and pressure turn limestone into marble.

# Activity: Comparing rocks

## What you will need

A magnifying glass, a steel nail, a pin or a piece of soft metal like copper, and some rocks.

You can collect rocks from almost anywhere, even on vacant lots in towns, or in your garden or, with permission, from parks. Samples can be picked up at the bottoms of cliffs or you can compare the rocks used for building such as limestone, or slate for roofs.

Make sure you have a good selection of rocks, including chalk and coal. Wet the surface of the rocks and see what colors there are. Use the magnifying glass to examine them. Are there crystals? Are the crystals different colors and sizes? What do the samples feel like? Are they smooth or are they made up of grains? Are they crumbly and easily broken?

Can you scratch them with your fingernail? Can they be scratched with a pin or the soft metal? Try to see if they can all be scratched by the steel nail.

## What did you see?

Did you find that your rocks are made up of many smaller particles? Igneous rocks can contain many differently colored crystals and have sharp jagged edges when broken. Most sedimentary rocks break with smoother edges and some will give a fine powder when scratched.

*This coastline shows two types of sedimentary rocks. The cliffs are made of layers of sandstone, while the rocks in the foreground are made of limestone.*

# 3. Crumbling the rocks

Soils are created partly by the breaking down of rocks into small particles. This is called weathering. Mechanical weathering includes the action of water, wind and temperature changes on the rock.

In wet, mountainous areas the cracks in rocks are filled with water. When water freezes it expands so that the ice takes up more space. The cracks are then made wider by the freezing process, eventually splitting the rock. The particles of rock in water will cause further weathering in the path of streams and rivers.

In dry places the rocks are heated to high temperatures during the day. When the Sun sets, though, the temperature falls quickly and the rapid cooling cracks the rock. The wind-driven soil will also scour the surface of rocks, like a sandblaster.

Plants and animals add to the weathering. For example, young trees will often take root in cracks in the rock. As the tree grows the pressure will force the rock apart.

Chemical weathering will also have an effect. Rainwater is a complex substance containing dissolved carbon dioxide, which turns into a weak acid (carbonic acid). This is natural acid rain. Limestone is made up mostly of calcium carbonate, which will not dissolve in pure water. However, the natural acid rain reacts with the calcium carbonate to give calcium bicarbonate, which will dissolve and be taken away in the water. The giant caves found within areas of limestone are caused by this.

*Wherever gritty particles are blown against rock surfaces there will be some erosion. This is particularly so in desert areas such as here in the Arches National Park, Utah.*

# Activity: Weathering in a freezer

## What you will need

A piece of limestone and a piece of sandstone, two plastic bags and the use of a freezer or the ice compartment of a refrigerator. Something to protect your hands from the cold, such as oven mitts, will be useful.

Soak the rocks in water for a day. Then put them each into a plastic bag and place them in the coldest part of a freezer. Leave them overnight. Then remove them carefully using the oven mitts since they will be very cold, and take them out of the bags.

Put each rock on a dish and let them thaw. This will take some time, so keep checking them during the day and write down what you see. You may need to repeat the experiment if there is no change. Which rock weathers the fastest?

## What did you see?

Was anything collected in the dishes? Where do you think this material came from? What happened to the water in the rock when it turned to ice? This is the way that many rocks are weathered to give the solid particles of the soil.

*The distinctive landscape of the Burren, in the Republic of Ireland, is due to the action of ice on the limestone.*

# 4. The rock in the soil

The tiny particles weathered from the rock are just the beginning of good soil, but they do play a part in making a particular kind of soil. If the particles are weathered from an acid rock, like granite, the soil will be acid. Similarly, if they are weathered from an alkaline rock, like limestone, the soil will be alkaline.

The size of the particles will also make a difference to the soil. The particle size may range from quite large, as in coarse sand, through fine sand and silt to the very small particles in clay.

The size of the particles affects the amount of air and water in the soil, and the speed with which water drains away. Sandy soil, which has quite big spaces between its large particles, has plenty of air in it, but does not hold water very well. However, the fine particles in clay soils hold water well so that clay does not drain very fast.

Water is needed in the soil to dissolve from the particles the elements from the particles that are required by the plants. Salts dissolve out of small particles more easily than from large ones because there is more surface for the water to reach. So, clay soils are usually richer in nutrient salts than sandy soils, because of their small particles.

Air is needed in the soil for the oxygen to combine with some of the elements used by the plants, and so that the bacteria can work. The bacteria are important in that they can free some of the essential materials used by the plants.

*This potato crop is growing in sandy soil.*

*This cherry orchard is supported by clay soil.*

# Activity: Soils and drainage

Put a small piece of filter paper in each pot to cover the holes and fill one with sand, the other with clay.

Stand each pot in a beaker. Pour equal amounts of water onto the soil in each pot and watch carefully to see how quickly the water drains through each.

Repeat this experiment for different types of soil and with some gravel. Each time use a new piece of filter paper and see how long it takes for the water to flow out.

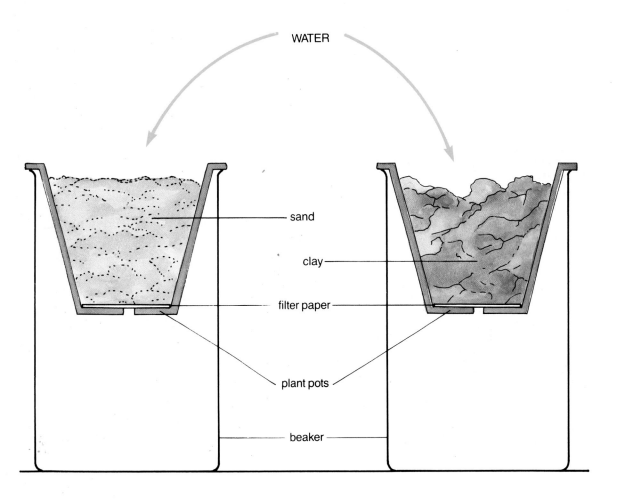

WATER

sand

clay

filter paper

plant pots

beaker

# 5. Soil and decay

Besides the weathering of rocks, the activity of plant and animal life (organisms) plays an essential part in the creation of soils. A cover of plants protects the soil so that it cannot be removed by the wind and the rain and the roots of plants grow into the soil and hold it together. In addition, when plants die their remains enrich the soil.

Bacteria, fungi, algae and simple one-celled animals feed on the remains of dead plants and animals. These living things are called decomposers and their feeding activity frees nutrients into the soil. These nutrients can then be taken in from the water in the soil by the roots of more complicated plants.

The waste remains of the plants and animals are called humus. The humus is an important part of the soil since it binds the minerals into small crumbly particles and makes the soil capable of holding more water.

The bacteria are the most important of the decomposers; a teaspoonful of soil may contain billions of them with different types breaking down different materials. Some types supply plants with such essential elements as nitrogen, in the form of nitrates, while others release carbon, in the form of carbon dioxide, from plant and animal remains. Still other microscopic soil life transforms such minerals as iron, manganese, sulphur and calcium and makes them available to plants.

Also present in vast numbers are tiny mites and simple wingless insects called springtails. They play an important part in breaking down the remains of plants, helping in the slow conversion of the litter of the forest floor into soil.

*Leaf litter on the floor of a Central American rain forest. The high temperatures and moisture in such an area are ideal for the rapid decaying of plant and animal remains.*

# Activity: Examining plant decay

## What you will need

Five plastic bags, a head of lettuce, rubber gloves, plenty of soil and some sand, rainwater or distilled water, five labels and a cardboard box. You will need the use of an oven.

## What did you see?

What has happened to the leaves? Have some decayed more quickly than others? What organisms are responsible for decay? Has the leaf that was in the baked soil decayed much? What do you think high temperatures do to the soil organisms?

Using the gloves, put a lettuce leaf in each of the bags. To the first bag add some dry soil to cover the leaf. In the second bag do this with sand. Bake some soil in a hot oven for several minutes and, when cool, add this to the third bag. In the fourth one add some soil that has been made very damp by the rainwater and leave the fifth bag empty except for the leaf. Label each bag clearly and close it tightly.

Put a layer of soil in the box and add the bags. Cover the bags with soil and leave them for a week. Then remove the bags and examine the leaves. Record any changes that you see.

Cover them up with the soil and wait another week before looking at the leaves again.

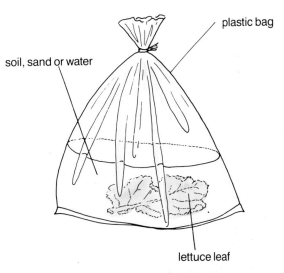

plastic bag

soil, sand or water

lettuce leaf

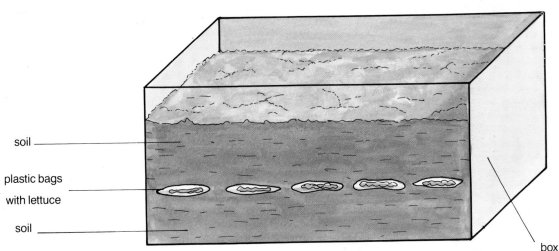

soil

plastic bags with lettuce

soil

box

# 6. The natural layers

Soils are not just a single layer of particles resting on top of the rocky crust. The soils vary with depth so that they slowly become divided into different layers, or "horizons." There are normally five horizons in the soil. If a slice is cut through undisturbed soil some of them can be seen. This slice is called a profile and each kind of soil has its own profile.

The top layer of the soil is called the O horizon. It does not contain any of the weathered rock particles, but consists of fresh or decaying organic material, such as leaves. Forest soils have a thick O horizon, desert soils do not have one.

The next layer is the A horizon. This is the topsoil, a dark mixture of organic material and soil particles. The dead remains are being broken down by soil animals and eaten by the decomposers. Most of the plant and animal life is in this layer, although long plant roots may grow deeper.

The middle layer is called the B horizon, or the subsoil. It contains many of the nutrients that have been washed down by the rain from the A horizon, as well as the remains of the humus.

The fourth layer, the C horizon, has no organic material in it. It is made from pieces of stone weathered from the parent material, the rock from which the minerals in the soil were removed. This material, the bedrock, may make up the bottom R horizon. Yet the parent material may have been brought from other places by moving ice, or rivers and seas or by the wind.

*A section through the soil to show the layers, or horizons.*

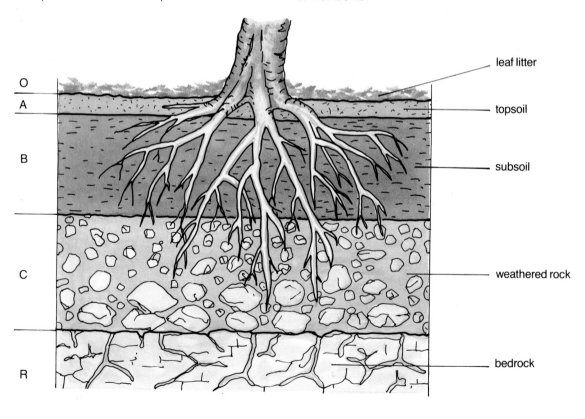

O
A

B

C

R

leaf litter

topsoil

subsoil

weathered rock

bedrock

# Activity: Solids in the soil

## What you will need

Two tall specimen tubes and corks, or two narrow beakers, a ruler and some garden soil from the surface and from about 40 or 50 cm (16 or 20 in) down. You may need a spade to dig down for this sample.

Quarter-fill one specimen tube with soil from the surface and add water until the tube is three-quarters full. Cover the top of the tube and shake it carefully but thoroughly and allow it to stand upright. Repeat this for some soil taken from below the surface.

Allow both tubes to stand for a while. Leave them overnight to obtain clearer results.

Look at the contents of the tubes and compare them. Are there different layers floating in the water and on the bottom of the tubes? Record the appearance of each layer. Use a ruler to measure the thickness of these layers for each tube and compare your results.

## What did you see?

Was there anything floating on the surface of the water? This is the humus, the decaying materials. Which has the most humus, soil from the surface or soil from well below ground level? Which has the coarser material in it?

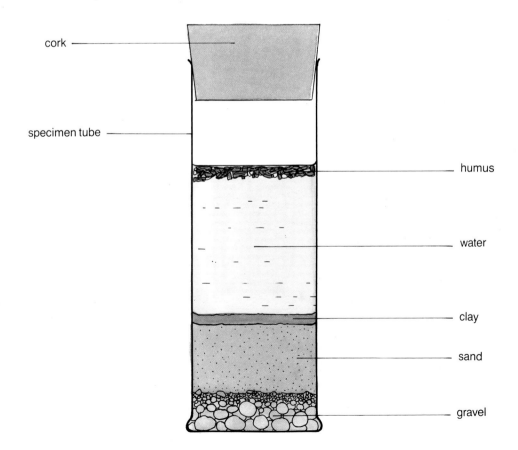

cork

specimen tube

humus

water

clay

sand

gravel

# 7. The soils of the planet

Different regions of the world have different soil types on which certain kinds of plants grow. How a soil develops is mostly influenced by the temperature, rainfall and material from which the soil particles were formed. The plant life will also have an effect.

In the north of Canada, Greenland and Siberia are found tundra soils, where the temperatures are very low. Here, lichens and mosses are joined by sedges, heathers and scrub such as willows, the soils having some humus in them. The C horizon is often permanently frozen.

Forest soils are much richer in humus. In coniferous forests the soils are acid since the plant materials decay into acids. Deciduous forest soils are less acidic and have plenty of nutrients. They support oaks, maples and chestnuts. In many parts of the world these forests have been cleared to give land for food crops.

The high temperatures and plentiful rainfall in tropical regions makes the soil organisms active, and plants grow, die and decay very quickly. There is a very shallow layer of humus in these soils which support the rain forests.

The prairie or grassland soils are formed in warm, fairly dry conditions like the North American prairies. Tall grasses grow naturally, but with enough rainfall food crops can be grown. Desert soils have little humus and are very dry, with a thin layer of subsoil over rock.

*Six typical soils are shown below.*

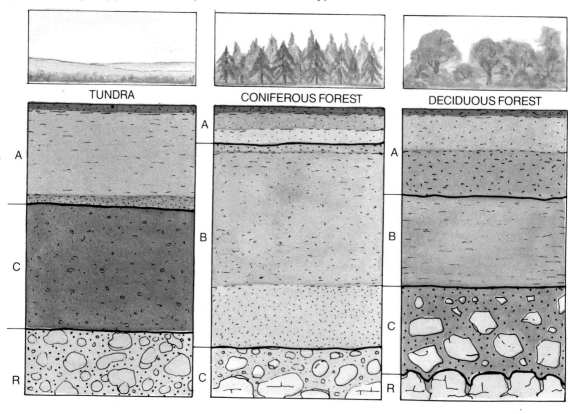

TUNDRA      CONIFEROUS FOREST      DECIDUOUS FOREST

# Activity: Acid and alkaline soils

## What you will need

Some distilled water, lime (calcium oxide), vinegar, beakers and some universal indicator solution, or papers, and the color chart provided with it. You will also need samples of soils from different areas. A sample from a chalky area and a sample of sandy soil from a marshy area would be good to test. Note the plant life growing in these areas.

The pH scale is used to measure how acid or alkaline a solution is. Distilled water has a pH of 7 and is neutral. An acid will have a pH of less than this, the lower the number the more acid the solution. An alkali will have a pH higher than 7.

Into two clean beakers add some distilled water and put a sample of each soil into them. Shake or stir them well and add the indicator. Record the pH numbers. What results do you get when you add lime to the acid solution?

First of all, make a solution of distilled water and vinegar. Test this with the indicator. What color do you see? Compare this with the colors on the chart and record the pH that is indicated. Add a little lime to the solution and shake. What do you see?

## What did you see?

Which was the most acid soil and which the alkaline one? How does the plant life in the two soils compare? Why do you think gardeners often "lime" the soil?

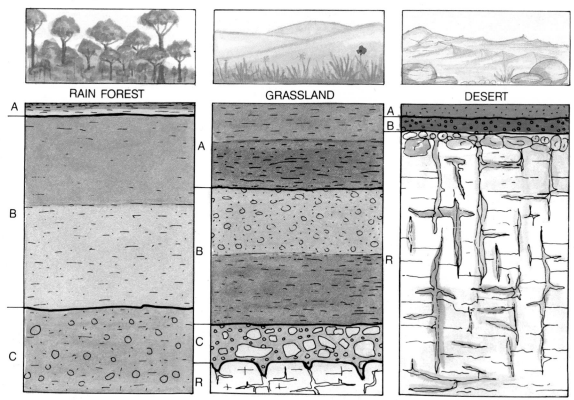

RAIN FOREST          GRASSLAND          DESERT

# 8. Plants and soil

Different plants grow in different soils. It is often possible to tell what a soil is like by the plants growing in it. Plants that grow in dry soils have small narrow leaves to prevent too much water loss by evaporation. Those in damp soils often have large leaves so they may lose excess water.

The part of a plant under the ground is sometimes as big as the part we can see. Below the surface of the soil there is a network of roots anchoring the plant to the soil. If a tree grows in, say, shallow soil, it will blow over in a strong wind when its roots cannot grow deep enough.

At the tip of each root there are very fine hairs that are small enough to move into the spaces

*The roots of this tree have been unable to penetrate the layer of chalk and have grown along the topsoil.*

between the soil particles. Here they find the water with the dissolved nutrients and take them in, so that the plant can use them to make food.

In areas of heavy rainfall the minerals and humus are washed through the topsoil and only plants with long roots can reach them. This is where forests grow. Where the nutrients remain near to the surface, grasses and plants with short roots grow.

Plants may also change the soil. Under a forest of deciduous trees, which drop their leaves in autumn, the soil is rich in humus from the decaying material and is well mixed by the great number of soil creatures. Coniferous trees have leaves all year round and their spiny leaves take a long time to decay, making the soil acid. Few animals like to live in this soil and so the material never gets well mixed.

# Activity: Growing a root system

## What you will need

Two glass plates and three sheets of blotting paper cut to the same size, some elastic bands, a tray of water, a broad bean seed and a corn kernel.

Cut a large hole in the center of each of two pieces of blotting paper. Lay one of these pieces on a glass plate and put a corn kernel in the middle of the hole. Put the whole piece of blotting paper over it. Place the broad bean seed in the center of this paper and position the second piece of blotting paper with the hole over the others. Lay the second plate on top and use elastic bands to secure the two plates firmly together.

Support this "sandwich" upright in a tray of water and examine the seeds each day. Keep a record of how they develop. Note how the roots and shoots appear. Look for any tiny root hairs.

## What did you see?

Do the seeds develop in the same way? Which part of them is different? Why do they grow in such different ways?

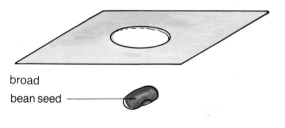

glass plate

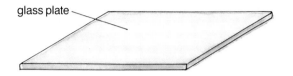

broad bean seed

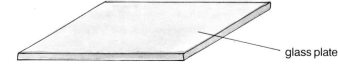

corn kernel

blotting paper

glass plate

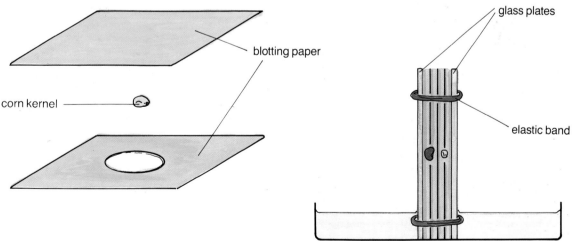

glass plates

elastic band

water

# 9. Underground animals

Life not only forms the soil, but incredible numbers of living things exist within it. If they did not then the soil would be dead and sterile. As well as the minute but hard-working life forms that are the decomposers, there are many larger creatures.

Some creatures spend all or most of their lives in the soil. The mole is an expert digger, having spade-like front paws to dig underground tunnels in its search for worms and slugs.

Other creatures come and go between the surface and the soil. Ants live in large groups, called colonies, and may be found in underground chambers where eggs are laid and where food is often stored. Rabbits also live in colonies. Their series of connecting burrows with many entrances are known as warrens. Feeding is done above ground but they shelter and give birth in the warren.

Still other creatures spend only certain parts of their lives in the soil. The cranefly lays its eggs in the soil and the larvae develop there, feeding on the roots of plants.

Many creatures spend the cold winter months in a long sleep called hibernation. The woodchuck will burrow as deep as 1.5 m (5 ft) to sleep over the winter in the ground, which is good at keeping the heat. Tortoises, snakes and frogs will also burrow into the soil before it freezes and the winter sets in. The few fish that hibernate also dig into the river bed.

*With its large claws the mole is an expert digger. This mole is eating a worm in its burrow.*

# Activity: Examining soil life

## What you will need

A spade or trowel, a ruler, a polyethylene bag, a magnifying glass, some white paper and a plastic covered dish or tray.

Find an area of soil that has not been disturbed. Mark off an area of about a foot square and dig out the soil down to about 10 cm (4 in) or more. Place the soil in a large polyethylene bag and take it indoors.

Spread the soil out on the white paper and use the magnifying glass to find any living things as you sift through the soil. Collect the animals and put them in the dish. Try to identify them and count their numbers. Compare the different types of life and how they move and feed. Remember to return them to the soil as soon as you can.

This is a good experiment to repeat at different times of the year on the same patch of land. You can also compare the number of animals in soil that has been disturbed.

## What did you see?

Were there many different types of soil creatures? Did you find any plant roots, seeds and decaying leaves as well?

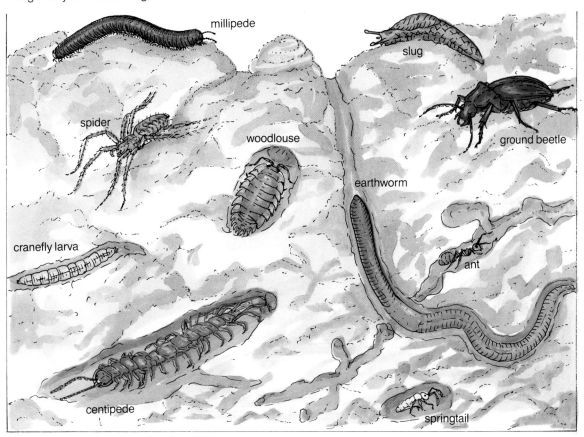

millipede

slug

spider

woodlouse

ground beetle

earthworm

cranefly larva

ant

centipede

springtail

*Some of the many examples of animal life to be found in the soil.*

# 10. The work of the earthworm

Of all the larger creatures in the soil, none are more important than the earthworms. They are found in great numbers on grassland and in chalky soil, with less in land that has been farmed and few in dry or waterlogged soil.

Worms feed mainly on decaying plant material. They tunnel through the earth, sometimes to depths of 6 m (19–20 ft), and this mixes the soil up and breaks it into finer pieces. This helps the decomposers to do their work more quickly.

*An earthworm with a worm casting.*

They eat their way through the A horizon, digesting the humus and passing the remains out behind them. Some pass this waste to the surface as worm castings and about 10 tons of soil can pass through such a worm each year.

In this way earthworms enrich the soil, passing nutrients to the topsoil. It was the naturalist Charles Darwin who first recognized the importance of earthworms and how they can efficiently bury things by bringing soil to the surface. Archaeologists at Stonehenge, in the UK, believe that worms raise the surface of the soil by about 15–20 cm (6–8 in) every 100 years.

As well as this, earthworms carry dead plant and animal remains from the surface into the lower layers of the soil where it may decay quickly. In addition, their burrows allow room for air in the soil, keep it well drained, and help plant roots to grow deeper.

*A section through the soil showing an earthworm in its burrow.*

# Activity: Make a worm terrarium

## What you will need

A small glass or clear plastic tank, plenty of fine garden soil and sandy soil, some dead leaves and some dark paper. You will also need to collect about ten earthworms.

Put the different soils in the tank in alternate layers, lightly moistening the soils with water as you do so. Gradually add the earthworms to different layers. On the surface place some small pieces of dead leaves. You have now made a worm terrarium. Draw how the layers appear so you have a record of what the terrarium looked like at the start of the experiment.

Cover the top of the terrarium with dark paper, punched with holes to allow air in, and keep a wrapper of dark paper around the tank so no light can reach in.

Leave the terrarium for a few days and then remove the paper and examine the soil layers and the leaves. Record any differences you see and then cover the tank with the paper. Examine the terrarium once or twice a week and keep a note of any changes.

## What did you see?

Why do you think alternate layers of soil were used? Have the layers changed? If so, what is responsible for this? What has happened to the leaves on top of the soil?

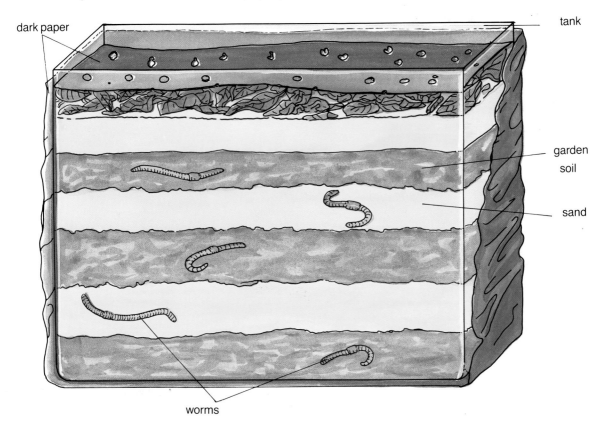

dark paper · tank · garden soil · sand · worms

# 11. Cycling the elements

Plants and animals need many chemical elements in order to live and grow. In living things these elements make up the cells and tissues of the body. Plants take the elements they need directly from the non-living world: the air, the water and the soil. The animals meet most of their needs by eating plants or other animals.

Life would quickly end if the vital elements were used just once, passing to the plants and animals, to disappear forever. To avoid this, the elements are cycled between the living and non-living world. Indeed, the food that you ate today was made from elements that have been used before.

The soil is in a state of constant change, taking part in cycles that have no beginning and no end. New materials are being added as rocks are broken up, as organic material decays and from the gases in the atmosphere. At the same time, other materials are being taken away by living creatures.

There are many different nutrient cycles. One of the most important is the nitrogen cycle. Nitrogen makes up some 78 percent of the air and all plants and animals need it for growth. Yet it is useless to plants when in the form of a gas. It has to be converted into a chemical that is called a nitrate before plants can use it.

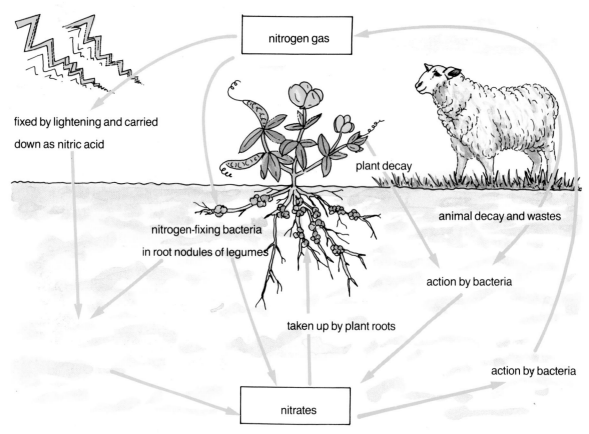

The complex nitrogen cycle. The gas is turned into a form that plants can take in and use for growth and pass on to animals.

*Alfalfa is grown on farm land to supply the soil with nitrogen.*

This is not an easy thing to do. A little of the gas is changed, or "fixed," by lightning during thunder storms, and is carried down in rain as nitric acid, where it enters the soil. Yet certain bacteria and some types of algae are responsible for "fixing" most of the nitrogen.

These nitrogen fixing bacteria live in the soil and in the roots of some plants. The legume family of plants, including clovers, sweet peas and alfalfas all have these bacteria living in small nodules in their roots. The nitrogen is converted into a nitrate that can be taken up by plant roots and used for growth. Animals will then be able to obtain the nitrogen by eating the plants. These animals will produce wastes and all living things will die and their remains decay. These also return the nitrogen to the soil where the bacteria can convert it again into a form to be of use to plants. Other types of bacteria will convert nitrates into nitrogen and release it into the atmosphere.

*The roots of this runner bean have many small nodules that contain bacteria. These bacteria "fix" nitrogen, converting it to a form that can be taken in by plants.*

# 12. Soil erosion

Since life has been on the planet for hundreds of millions of years, the soil covering the rock should be very deep. However, in some places the rock has no soil cover at all. Wind and water both help to make soil, but they can also destroy it by carrying the topsoil away.

The erosion, or wearing away, of the soil is slowed down if it is covered by a protective layer of plants. Growing plants bind the soil together with their roots, so water trickling through does not wash away the soil particles. Leaves and stems also protect the soil from heavy rain and wind.

People are also responsible for wearing away the soil. Farmers uncover the soil when they plow the land, and the cutting down of trees for industry and fuel exposes the topsoil. For example, the extensive removal of the forest cover in the Himalayan foothills has led to huge quantities of topsoil being carried the long distance to the mouth of the Ganges River.

It is not just poor countries that suffer from erosion. Experts have calculated that in the past 200 years the U.S. has lost about one-third of its farming land due to soil erosion.

Soil erosion can be prevented, however. For instance, farmers can reduce erosion due to water by plowing across the shape of a hillside instead of down it, or by building terraces, or steps, up the hillside. This keeps the rain from washing the soil downhill.

*Building terraces on hillsides to prevent erosion by running water is not a recent invention. These rice terraces in the Philippines are 2,000 years old.*

# Activity: Water on the soil

## What you will need

Two cardboard boxes, sheets of polyethylene, bricks and some garden soil. You will also need a watering can or a garden hose.

It is best to perform this experiment out of doors. Cut one end of the narrow ends from each box and line it with the polyethylene. Fill both boxes with loose garden soil and tilt them both equally on bricks so that the cut-away ends are in contact with the ground.

Make furrows with a stick up and down the dirt in one box and across the dirt slope in the other. Spray equal amounts of water on both and watch what happens.

Allow the soil to drain and then use more bricks to lift up the ends farther. Again spray both soils with water and watch what happens.

## What did you see?

How did the water run off the soil? Was much soil removed by the water? Was there a difference when the soil was steeper? What does this tell you about methods of plowing and sowing seeds on steeply sloping ground?

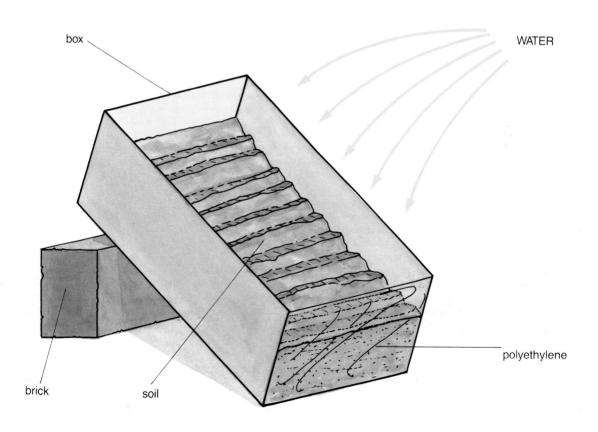

box

WATER

brick

soil

polyethylene

# 13. Changing the land

People first began to grow their own food about 10,000 years ago. It was discovered that seeds could be sown to provide a crop in land near to their homes.

The planting of seeds in holes or trenches and the removal of weeds were the first steps in cultivation. Cultivation means the preparation of land so that the crops are sown quickly and have a good chance of growing. Tools like the hand-hoe and the plow were invented to help in the cultivation of the land.

When the numbers of people were small, farmers could move to new lands when their old fields were exhausted, cutting down forests and burning the vegetation to make way for their crops. As the population grew the way of growing crops changed to make better use of the land and to feed the people in the growing towns.

A method developed whereby the land was divided up for different crops and each crop

*A woman guiding a plow across the land in Tunisia. In the poorer nations of the world it is women who perform most of the agricultural work, sometimes including plowing.*

changed, or rotated, every year. One field was left without a crop, or fallow, so it could recover. This fallow land was planted with crops that replenished the soil. Clover, for example, put nitrates back into the soil and was used for animals to graze.

It was then discovered that the soil could be improved by adding rotting vegetation and old bones to it, and from this fertilizers developed. With the industrial revolution 200 years ago machines were invented to plow and harvest the land, changing the face of the countryside forever. Now, chemical fertilizers are widely used and other chemicals control weeds and pests, with much land intensively cultivated. Yet such modern methods are not without their problems.

# Activity: Fertilizer and soil

## What you will need

Three small pots of the same size, some radish seeds or wheat grains and some sand. You will also need a little fertilizer or compost.

Fill the first pot with sand. Half fill the second pot with sand and then add the same amount of fertilizer on top. Into the third pot add the same amounts of sand and fertilizer but mix them thoroughly together. Label each pot.

Plant two or three seeds in each pot, just below the surface, and lightly water. Examine the pots each day and keep a record of the growth of the plants. Note the color, number and size of the leaves in each pot.

## What did you see?

How did the plants in each pot compare? In what ways do fertilizers improve the growth of plants?

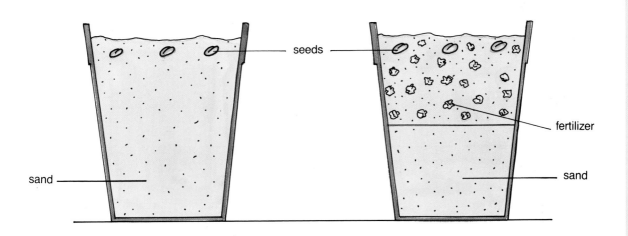

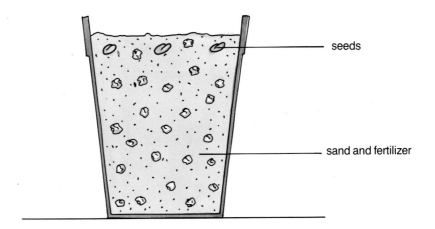

# 14. The problems of agriculture

Our modern ways of farming produce as much food as possible from the land for humans and their animals. The growing of crops is intended for the benefit of humans only, unlike the natural world where food is cycled among all the living things.

The soil can easily become exhausted when it is farmed but the natural vegetation does not do this. The reason is that the natural plants live and die in the same place. Only a small number of plants are eaten, and the rest decay, freeing the nutrients into the soil so they can be taken in again by other plants.

The crops humans grow are often completely cut down at harvesting time and taken away. The precious nutrients go with them and the parts that are left in the field are often burnt to kill any plant diseases. So there is no recycling of the vital nutrients, and the quality of the soil is reduced.

*The intensive plowing of fields can increase the problems of soil erosion, as here in the foothills of mountains in Baja California.*

The nutrients can be replaced by adding fertilizers to the soil. Instead of natural fertilizers like manure, chemical fertilizers have been created. Sometimes far too much fertilizer is used and can be washed from the soil by the rain to pollute the underground water, rivers, lakes and eventually end up in drinking water.

Modern farming also uses powerful chemicals called pesticides to kill insects, animals, weeds and diseases that would damage the crops. All pesticides are dangerous to something, otherwise they would be of no use, and such chemicals, including the infamous DDT, have accidentally caused much harm to wildlife. One of the main problems is that a creature may eat another that has taken in the

*Spraying a pesticide on a growing crop. There is much concern that traces of these chemicals have ended up in human food.*

pesticide and the chemicals can pass along the food chain. Birds of prey have been particularly affected and there is concern that traces of pesticides have found their way into human food.

Both fertilizers and pesticides are expensive and as the quality of the soil falls, more and more chemicals are needed. An alternative to this would be to regularly change the crops in different fields, which naturally increases the fertility and reduces pests. Animal and human waste could also be used to enrich the soil and the natural enemies of certain pests could be deliberately introduced.

# 15. The spreading deserts

The world has always had its deserts, dry areas where there is little rain and few plants and animals. Yet never before have new ones been created quite as fast as now. About one-third of the Earth's land surface is desert or near-desert with 700 million people living in them. Yet much of this land, amounting to one-fifth of the planet's surface, is threatened by the spread of the deserts.

The spreading deserts affect rich and poor countries alike. Some 10 percent of the United States has already been affected and a further 20 percent is threatened. But the world's attention has been drawn to the famines in the Sahel and Sudan regions of Africa as the Sahara has spread to the south.

Why are the deserts spreading? No one is quite sure whether or not there is less rainfall in these regions, but it seems that the speed with which they are increasing has little to do with a change in the climate. Indeed, it is not that the deserts are expanding, but that the land near them is getting poorer and can support less and less agriculture.

The removal of more trees than are planted is probably one of the main reasons since trees keep the soil fertile, hold moisture and prevent erosion. Across the world, people are forced to cut down trees since they are desperate for fuel.

*These women in Somalia are carrying brushwood to be planted in the sand. This will stabilize the dunes and keep them from spreading.*

Attempts to increase food production is another reason. Livestock are essential for meat and milk but they eat young seedlings and prevent the growth of new plant life. Shrubs are also often cut down to provide food for the animals. This makes the soil more likely to be eroded. There is now such pressure to increase crop production that leaving the land fallow for a period is often forgotten and very intensive methods are used. All these take their toll on the land.

Much effort is being made to reclaim the land that is lost and to halt the deserts' spread. Irrigation has been thought of as the best way of reclaiming the driest lands by bringing in a water supply. However, such schemes can easily add to the problem. The land may become waterlogged if there is not enough drainage and since water evaporates quickly from the soil, the mineral salts are brought to the surface by the water. Some crops grow

*This plantation of trees stabilizes sand dunes in Brazil.*

well in salty soils, but most cannot.

Many deserts receive enough rain for vegetation but plants cannot take root since the soil is easily eroded. Farm lands may be created by growing certain types of plants and drought-resistant trees to protect the land from the wind. The sand dunes are then "stabilized," allowing other plants to grow.

There is another type of desert that is spreading. Much of the world's land is being covered by concrete. The need for roads and houses, factories and airports has resulted in the loss of about six million hectares (14.8 million areas) of good land in the last ten years. In the poorer nations some of the best land is turning into desert, but in the richer countries, it is turning into pavement.

# 16. Energy from the land

The land contains many sources of energy that can be tapped. Most notable are the fossil fuels. These were formed from the remains of long-dead plants and animals. The energy stored up in them when they were alive is released as heat when we burn fuels like coal and gas.

The solid fossil fuel is coal. It was formed when giant ferns and other now-extinct plants fell into acid swamps that prevented their decay. The plants became covered by layers of sand or mud and were gradually broken down and pressed into peat. The pressure due to movements of the Earth's crust and heat finally produced the coal we use today.

It took very large forests and millions of years to make the coal we burn for electricity and heat and the reserves of this fuel will not last

*A steam well in Iceland. The heat within the Earth is near enough to the surface to be used to heat homes and factories.*

*This huge machine digs over 2,000 tons of coal per hour from the face of a mine in the state of Victoria, Australia.*

forever. Yet, some experts think that we have enough left for 200 years or more. The burning of coal has dangers as well since gases are released, some of which add to the "acid rain" problem, and to the "greenhouse effect."

Oil and natural gas are the other fossil fuels. They were formed from the remains of plants and tiny sea creatures that were buried in mud on the seabed. As in the formation of coal, pressure and heat turned the remains into gas and oil. However, some experts think these sources will be used up in 50 years.

The Earth has another source of energy. Under the planet's crust the core is very hot indeed and in some places hot water and steam shoot up through faults in the crust as geysers. Iceland has tapped its hot waters to heat its towns, and several other countries, such as New Zealand, are also using this energy source to turn turbines and produce electricity.

# 17. Dumping the wastes

Humans are a very wasteful species. Since the Stone Age people have left behind piles of chipped flints, shells, pottery and bones that archaeologists uncover and explore. So the dumping of everyday trash, called domestic waste, is not a new activity.

Today, the disposal of garbage is costly. The expense of collecting the waste and transporting it to a dump is high and natural resources such as metals and wood are lost. Most refuse is piled outside towns on dumps. The decaying organisms can break down some of this waste, which is called biodegradable. Plastics, however, are bad for the environment since they are non-biodegradable; they do not decompose.

*Household refuse on a dump. Such places support many scavenging animals, including gulls.*

*The wastes of an industry dumped onto moorland in Britain. This is a pile of china clay waste left over from the manufacture of ceramics.*

Some towns have recognized this wastage of land and materials; the rubbish they sort so that valuable materials such as paper, glass and the metals in tin cans may be extracted and used again, or "recycled." Even plastic containers can now be used to make a fuel for use in industry.

The land may also be affected by industry. The wastes left over from mining and industrial processes may build up in dumps, giving an ugly appearance to the landscape and sometimes affecting the vegetation. Attempts have been made to cover unsightly dumps with plants and trees and to fill in the old quarries.

More worrying is the dumping of harmful materials. Chemical wastes are often buried and may poison the land and the water draining through it so that the poisons are passed on to fish, birds of prey and even people. Dealing with the radioactive wastes from the nuclear industry is another area causing concern. Some is buried in containers, but the underground water would be polluted if the containers leaked.

# 18. Conserving the land

The soil is one of our most precious resources. It is the store of the elements that are an important part of every living thing, and we must realize just how essential it is. Plants cannot grow properly without these elements. They need such substances as iron and magnesium to help make their chlorophyll, the chemical that traps the Sun's energy, and enables them to make their own food. It is this food that all animals, including humans, depend on.

Yet the quality of the soil is getting worse because people did not think about the results of filling in sites with hazardous wastes, or farming the land for the maximum profit.

Most people are becoming better informed about the problems facing the environment simply because such matters are becoming news, and many of the problems are appearing closer to home. Many people know of hazardous waste sites near where they live and are willing to protest about them and the creation of new ones.

All over the world the topsoil is being lost through erosion. Fierce rains wash away the soil and cut deep gullies on recently farmed hillsides. Winds can turn valuable topsoil into clouds of dust. As farmers go into debt and their crops and livestock fetch lower prices, they often need to put survival ahead of soil conservation.

The soil of a country is one of its most vital resources, but as farmers plow more fragile lands like prairies and steep hillsides which are easily eroded, more soil is lost. In the U.S. alone, the government believes that about 3,000 million tons of soil is stripped from the nation's farmland each year.

The United States is one of the countries with a Soil Conservation Service, whose task is to inform the nation of the problems of erosion and to suggest ways to protect the soil. Governments have made laws to take easily

*This land was once an industrial waste site. Now it has been reclaimed and turned into an area of parkland.*

eroded land out of production for several years and to replant it with grass and trees so that it can recover. Farmers have also been encouraged to use different methods of farming that help to conserve the soil.

Land that is essential for rare wildlife is also being lost as mining and mineral companies move in to dig for fuel and other valuable

*These volunteers are stabilizing a loose trail on a mountainside. This will ensure the regrowth of plant life to stop erosion.*

products of the Earth. Laws can help to preserve some of these vital lands and can ensure that the waste products of mining and industry are covered with earth and replanted.

# Glossary

**Acid rain** Rain is normally slightly acid. But gases like the oxides of sulphur and nitrogen, which are released into the air by burning fuels like coal, dissolve in the water in the air and fall as acid rain, snow or mist.

**Algae** A major group of plants of very simple form. They contain chlorophyll but lack stems, roots and leaves.

**Atmosphere** The layer of gases that surround a planet, held there by gravity.

**Bacteria** Extremely small living things that bring about the decay of plant and animal remains and wastes.

**Bedrock** The solid, unweathered rock that lies beneath the soil.

**Biodegradable** Able to be decomposed so that the elements from which something is made can return to the land.

**Carbonic acid** The natural acid that forms in the air when carbon dioxide reacts with water vapor.

**Clay** A fine-grained soil.

**Coniferous Trees** Trees that have cones instead of flowers.

**Crop** Plants grown on cultivated land; for example cereals, vegetables and fruit.

**Crust** The surface "skin" of the Earth.

**Cultivate** To prepare land for crops, tend the plants and harvest them.

**Darwin, Charles** naturalist (1809–82) who first investigated the importance of earthworms and who is best known for his theory of evolution.

**DDT** A colorless substance used to control insect pests on crops. It is poisonous to animals and builds up in the body.

**Decay** To rot as a result of the action of bacteria or fungi.

**Deciduous Trees** Trees that shed their leaves at the end of the growing season.

**Decomposer** An organism that breaks down the bodies of dead plants and animals into simple substances.

**Desert** A region where there is little rainfall and few plants and animals.

**Ecology** The study of how living things affect, and are affected by, their environment.

**Environment** The world around us, or our surroundings, including all living things. The place where an animal or plant lives may be called its environment.

**Erosion** The wearing away, or weathering, of the land surface.

**Evaporation** The change of a liquid into a vapor.

**Fallow Land** Land left without a crop so that it can regain its fertility.

**Fertilizer** A substance containing plant foods used to increase the fertility of the soil and thus the quantity of the crops.

**Food chain** A chain of living things through which energy is passed as food.

**Fossil** The impression of a plant or animal that has been dead for millions of years. Fossils are found in certain types of rocks.

**Fossil fuels** Those fuels (oil, gas and coal) that have been formed in the ground over millions of years from the decay of once living things.

**Fungi** Simple plants that do not contain chlorophyll. They take their food from dead or living plants and animals.

**Geyser** A spring that throws a jet of hot water and steam into the air. Geysers only occur in volcanic regions and can be used to generate electricity.

**Greenhouse effect** A condition in which carbon dioxide and other gases cause heat to be trapped in the atmosphere and prevented from escaping back into space.

**Hibernate** To sleep over the winter months.

**Hoe** Hand- or machine-held implement to break up the soil.

**Horizon** A specific layer of the soil.

**Humus** The decaying plant and animal remains found in soil.

**Igneous rock** A rock that has solidified from molten magma.

**Irrigation** The bringing in of water by artificial means to a dry area.

**Larvae** The grubs that develop into insects.

**Lava** Molten rock or magma that has been forced to the surface in a volcanic eruption.

**Lichen** A type of plant consisting of an alga living in a fungus. Lichens are found as crusty patches or bushy growths.

**Magma** The molten rock that forms below the solid rock of the Earth's crust, and can reach the surface as lava.

**Mantle** The layer of the Earth that is between the crust and the core.

**Microscopic** Not large enough to be seen with the naked eye but visible under a microscope.

**Minerals** The materials in rocks, which are needed to build up the foods in plants.

**Nitrates** Chemicals containing nitrogen, which is needed by plants.

**Nitrogen** The gas that makes up about 78 percent of the air.

**Nitrogen cycle** The circulation of nitrogen from the air to the soil, plants and animals, and back to the air.

**Organism** Any plant or animal.

**Oxygen** The gas that makes up nearly 21 percent of the air. It is essential for life.

**Pesticides** Chemicals used for killing pests like insects and rodents.

**pH scale** The scale that measures how acid or alkaline a substance is. Pure water has a pH of seven. Acids have a pH of less than this and alkalis have a higher pH.

**Pollution** The release of substances into the air, water or land that may upset the natural balance of the environment. Such substances are called pollutants.

**Prairie** A treeless grassy plain of the central U.S. and southern Canada.

**Radioactive** Giving out harmful rays.

**Rain forest** A dense forest found in the hot, tropical areas of the world.

**Recycling** Passing a substance through a system in order to be used again.

**Root** The part of a plant that is usually underground and absorbs water and minerals from the soil. It also acts as an anchor.

**Sedimentary rocks** The rocks formed when sand, soil and mud were pressed together.

**Sial** The upper layer of the crust of the planet, rich in silica and aluminum.

**Sima** The lower layer of the Earth's crust, rich in silica and magnesia.

**Topsoil** The dark, top layer of the soil, with much humus.

**Tundra** A type of cold, treeless plain found in Arctic lands.

**Vegetation** The plant life of a particular area.

**Weathering** The erosion of rocks and soil by rain, wind, ice and the heat of the Sun.

# Further information

## Books to read

*City and Suburb: Exploring an Ecosystem*, by Laurence Pringle. Macmillan, 1975.

*Deciding How to Live on Spaceship Earth*, by Rodney F. Allen, *et al*. McDougall-Littel, 1973.

*Discovering Worms*, by J. Couldry, Bookwright Press, 1986.

*Finding out about Conservation*, by John Bentley and Bill Charlton. David and Charles, 1983.

*Flowering Plants*, by Alfred Leutscher. Franklin Watts, 1985.

*The Future of the Environment*, by Mark Lambert. Bookwright Press, 1986.

*How Life on Earth Began*, by William Jaspersohn. Franklin Watts, 1985.

*Poisoned Land: The Problem of Hazardous Waste*, by Irene Kiefer. Atheneum, 1981.

*Pollution*, by Geraldine Woods and Harold Woods. Franklin Wattts, 1983.

*Story of the Ice Age*, by Gerald Ames and Rose Wyler. Harper and Row, 1956.

*Understanding Ecology*, rev. ed. by Elizabeth T. Billington. Frederick Warne & Co., 1971.

*Volcanoes and Earthquakes*, by Martyn Bramwell. Franklin Watts, 1986.

*A Walk in the Forest: The Woodlands of North America*, by Albert List, Jr. and Ilka List. Crowell Junior Books, 1977.

## Organizations to contact

The following organizations will provide further information including leaflets, posters and project packs, and there may be a local group for you to join. Remember to send a stamped addressed envelope with all inquiries.

**Audubon Naturalist Society of the Central Atlantic States**
8940 Mill Road
Chevy Chase, Maryland 20815
301–652–9188

**Children of the Green Earth**
P.O. Box 200
Langley,Washington, 98260
206–321–5291

**Clean Water Action Project**
317 Pennsylvania Avenue, S.E.
Washington, D.C. 20003
202–547–1196

**Conservation Foundation**
1717 Massachusets Avenue, N.W.
Washington, D.C. 20036
202–797–4300

**Environmental Action Foundation**
1525 New Hampshire Avenue, N.W.
Washington, D.C. 20036
02–745–4870

**Environmental Defense Fund**
257 Park Avenue South, Suite 16
New York, New York 10016
212–686–4191

**Greenpeace, USA**
1611 Connecticut Avenue, N.W.
Washington, D.C. 20009
202–462–1177

**National Parks and Conservation Association**
1701 18th Street, N.W.
Washington, D.C. 20009
202–265–2717

**National Wildlife Federation**
1412 16th Street, N.W.
Washington, D.C. 20036
202–797–6800

**The Nature Conservancy**
1800 North Kent Street, Suite 800
Arlington, Virginia 2220
703–841–8300

**World Watch Institute**
1776 Massachusets Avenue, N.W.
Washington, D.C. 20036
202–452–1999

**World Wildlife Fund**
1255 23rd Street, N.W.
Washington, D.C. 20037
202–293–4800

# Index

## Picture acknowledgments

The author and publishers would like to thank the following for allowing their illustrations to be reproduced in this book: David Bowden Picture Library *frontispiece*; Bruce Coleman Limited *cover* (left B. & C. Calhoun, right A. Deere-Jones), 8 (O. Drayton), 10 (B. & C. Calhoun), 27 (bottom A. Davies), 32 (F. Lanting), 35 (L.C. Marigo), 39 (C. Molyneux); Jimmy Holmes Himalayan Images 41; Cecilia Fitzsimons 7, 13, 15, 16, 17, 18–19, 21, 23, 25, 26, 29, 31; G.S.F. Picture Library 12 (both), 28, 38; Oxfam 34, Oxford Scientific Films 6 (G. Merlen), 9 (P. O'Toole), 14, 22, 24 (left), 27 (top) (D.H. Thomson), 20 (S. Foote), 37 (M.F. Chillmaid), 40 (T.C. Middleton); Zefa Picture Library 30 (Knight & Hunt Photo) 33 (G. Kalt). All other illustrations from Wayland Picture Library.